#2

Excuses Are Your Destiny

Destiny S. Harris

. . .

. . .

Copyright

. . .

A Gift For You

Thank you for taking the time to read this book. As a token of my appreciation, here is a gift to you.

I give away free books daily. Here's how to get your free books today:

Step 1: Visit amazon.com/author/destinyharris

Step 2: Filter books by "Price: Low to High"

Step 3: Download available free eBooks

. . .

. . .

Table of Contents

. . .

. . .

Quick Bit

Thank you for taking the time to read this book.

My hope is that you leave at least 1% better than before you read this book and walk away with at least one takeaway.

I'd like to graciously ask that you help me by leaving a <u>review</u> of this book; your feedback helps me write better books and helps others get a glimpse of the book.

With Kindness,
Destiny

. . .

...

Excuses Are Your Destiny

People who make excuses will never get far in life.

Excuses are your destiny.

Too Tired

"I can't do x because I don't have time."

Who isn't tired? We all experience moments of exhaustion, stress, and low energy. But it is in these moments that we must push through the most.

The most challenging moments to work on our goals are the best moments to work on our goals; these moments develop us into refined human beings.

It's easy to work on your goals and your life when you're energetic...not so much when you're tired as fuck.

Fuck your exhaustion and get to work -- even if it's only one rep. A little effort goes a long way when you're consistent.

...

...

Not Motivated

"I can't do x because I don't feel like it."

If you're waiting to be motivated to work on your goals, you might be waiting for the rest of your life because motivation is not something that just happens daily.

Mastery only comes to those who can push through times when they're not motivated, which is probably 75% or more of the time, unless you're very lucky.

Don't wait to be motivated. Instead, create motivation through consistency. The more consistent you are, the more your efforts compound and build a mountain of momentum.

Momentum is the most reliable motivator.

. . .

. . .

Depressed

"I can't do x because I'm feeling low."

Some of the most depressed people are the same people who don't consistently work on their goals and dreams.

When you're not working on your goals and dreams, you're living life without purpose -- without aim.

A person who lives without purpose is drifting. It's easy to get caught up with unproductive emotions while living aimlessly.

Step outside of your depression into the light by getting outside of yourself.

Want to know an easy way to get outside of yourself? Do something generous for someone else. Better yet, dive into a purpose that fulfills your spirit and positively impacts the lives of others. It's hard to be depressed when you're consistently adding value to others.

. . .

No Time

"I can't do x because I don't have time."

Some people have more open schedules than others. But the crazy thing is when I see parents carry a full-time job, have a full-time school schedule, and manage a full set of kids. Some people do 10x or more than these parents, too.

Everyone has a load of shit they carry on their shoulders.

Everyone is "busy" and has sh*t to do, but we all get the same 24 hours a day.

It's what you do with your time that matters most.

If you don't have time, start waking up earlier, give up social media, give up television, give up socializing, and give up anything that is impeding progress on your goals.

Furthermore, **subtract** from your life. The fewer responsibilities and obligations you have to maintain, the more availability you have for other things (the things that matter most).

You got time. Stop lying to yourself. Eradicate the superfluous.

. . .

Victimization

"I can't do x because y happened to me, or w did that to me."

Life moves forward even when you don't.

If you remain in the past, your life will revolve indefinitely in the same direction.

Do you like the direction your life is headed? If not, what you're doing today isn't going to take you any steps further.

"I can't take care of myself because I care for everyone else."

"I don't have time to get a new job because my current schedule takes up all my time."

"I can't leave this relationship because no one else will love me. I've been here too long, so I might as well stay."

"I can't leave this town; I've lived here all my life."

"I can't switch careers; I've committed so much time, effort, and resources to my current career."

"I can't do that. Imagine what people will think of me."

Victims allow everything and every one to dictate their outcomes; they always give their power away, which is why they never position themselves to overcome anything or make much progress in life.

When you stay a victim, don't expect your life to improve.

. . .

...

Your Circumstances

"I can't do x because I have to do a, b, c, d, e, and f -- not to mention g."

If you keep up this narrative, guess where you'll be ten years from now?

It's the exact place you're in now.

Your circumstances can only dictate your results if you allow them to.

There will always be an impediment that makes your journey from A to Z more challenging; the barriers make the journey worthwhile. When you get to the finish line, you're not supposed to be the same person at the starting line.

Never allow your circumstances to dictate your outcomes. Push through your barriers. Push through the pain. Push through the "no's". Push through the opposition.

Circumstances are supposed to **make you,** not break you and dim your life results.

. . .

Thank You For Reading

Thank you for reading this book.

Stay loved, blessed, lucky, favored, aware, joyous, enlightened, and committed to bettering yourself.

...

...

The End.

. . .

. . .

About Destiny S. Harris

Destiny S. Harris' goal is to positively inspire, cultivate, elevate, and educate the minds of individuals across the globe through her writing.

Creating (whether books, courses, articles, poetry, or music) has always been Destiny's thing, not to mention health & fitness and all things entrepreneurial.

Destiny published her first book, "Beauty Secrets for Girls," at age 11 and her second book, "Don't Wait Until It's Too Late," at age 12.

Destiny obtained three degrees in Psychology, Political Science, & Women's Studies. She also started her own music teaching business at the age of 14, which she led for over ten years. In addition, she has been teaching academic, career, and personal development topics to thousands of students and readers since 2004.

Outside of writing, Destiny loves and enjoys many activities: reading, weightlifting, walking, biking, traveling, football (and sports in general), dogs, animals, food, classic movies, quality and new experiences, mountain, and ocean views, sleeping, plants, and nature.

Check out her work, leave a review, share your thoughts with your friends and family, and participate in a movement: **Serving others through self-education (books).**

<u>**Complete the Steps To Get Free eBooks:**</u>

Step 1: Go to

amazon.com/author/destinyharris

Step 2: Filter books by "Price: Low to High"

Step 3: Download available free books

. . .

. . .

Connect W/ Destiny S. Harris

Please reach out and stay in touch. Start a conversation today @ destinyh.com

. . .

. . .

Free Gifts!

Access courses & free eBooks at the link below:

destinyh.com

...

Please Leave A Review

If this book impacts you in some way, please let me know by dropping a review on it.

I write better books with **your** input.

. . .

Tell Me What You Want

I've written many books, but if you don't see what you're looking for or need, get in touch with me via my website, articles, comments, or reviews, and let me know what you're looking for so I can create it for you. I'm here to serve.

Destiny

. . .

...